SPOTTER'S GUIDE TO
DOGS

Harry Glover

Illustrated by John Francis and Andy Martin

Americanization: Carrie Seay
US expert: Reed Keffer

Edited by Alastair Smith, Rosamund Kidman Cox and Tim Dowley
Designed by Karen Tomlins and Joanne Kirkby
Digital illustrations by Verinder Bhachu
Cover and series designer: Laura Fearn
Consultant: Hazel Palmer

Cover © Jane Burton; p.1 © Robert Dowling/Corbis;
p.2-3 © Jim Richardson/Corbis; p.5 © Robert Dowling/Corbis;
p.6-7 © Yann Arthus-Bertrand/Corbis; p.56 © Kevin R. Morris/Corbis;
p.58-59 © Joe McDonald/Corbis.

First published in 2001 by Usborne Publishing Ltd.,
Usborne House, 83-85 Saffron Hill, London, EC1N 8RT, England.
www.usborne.com
This edition first published in America in 2003.

AE. Printed in Spain

CONTENTS

HOW TO USE THIS BOOK

This book is an identification guide to dog breeds. Take it with you whenever you are likely to see dogs – whether you go out walking, to the park or to a dog show.

Originally, most dog breeds were developed to do a certain job. In this book the breeds are arranged into groups according to the jobs for which they were used.

Next to each picture is a short description of the breed. It tells you where the breed originated, its coloring, temperament and height.

There is a chart on pages 62-63. It lists all the breeds featured in this book. When you spot a certain breed, jot down the date that you saw it on the chart. You'll soon build a record of the breeds that you've spotted.

Name of breed	Date
Otterhound	8/6
Papillon	8/6
Pekingese	5/7
Pinscher, Miniature	10/11
Pointer	10/11

Fill in the chart like this.

When you spot a breed, make a mark in the circle next to its picture.

4

DOG BREEDING

Dogs have been bred for thousands of years – originally to make types that were suited to particular purposes, such as hunting, pulling sleds or guarding. Today's dog breeds started in this way.

Today, dogs are bred more for their beauty than for their qualities as working dogs. However, many retain their ancestors' instincts. For example, a dog that was originally bred to hunt things will tend to chase other animals.

Originally, Dalmatians were bred for stamina. Today, they are bred just for their looks, but they have the same boundless energy as their ancestors.

LOOKING AT DOGS

Dogs and their body parts are described with particular words. The most important ones are shown on this picture of a beagle.

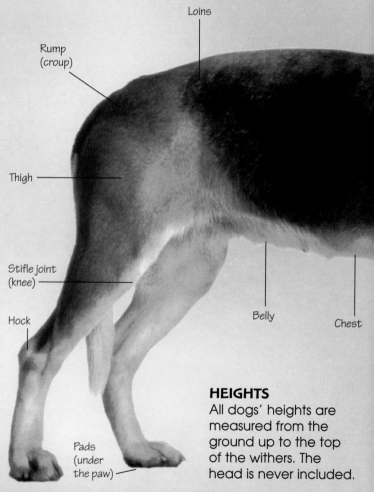

Loins

Rump
(croup)

Thigh

Stifle joint
(knee)

Hock

Belly

Chest

Pads
(under
the paw)

HEIGHTS
All dogs' heights are measured from the ground up to the top of the withers. The head is never included.

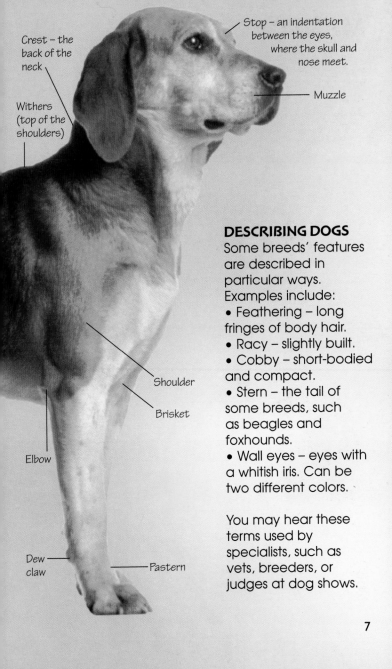

Crest – the back of the neck

Stop – an indentation between the eyes, where the skull and nose meet.

Muzzle

Withers (top of the shoulders)

Shoulder

Brisket

Elbow

Dew claw

Pastern

DESCRIBING DOGS
Some breeds' features are described in particular ways. Examples include:
• Feathering – long fringes of body hair.
• Racy – slightly built.
• Cobby – short-bodied and compact.
• Stern – the tail of some breeds, such as beagles and foxhounds.
• Wall eyes – eyes with a whitish iris. Can be two different colors.

You may hear these terms used by specialists, such as vets, breeders, or judges at dog shows.

7

MARKINGS

Occasionally, the names given to dogs' markings are unusual, and don't give much of a clue as to what the animal's coat really looks like. These pictures explain some of the more unusual names.

Black and tan Blue Brindle Bronze

Buff Chestnut Grizzle Harlequin

Liver Merle and white Mouse-gray Pied

Roan Salt and pepper Tricolor Wheaten

TAILS

When you are identifying breeds, look at the tails. Some breeds hold theirs in a distinctive way, as shown here.

Tails come in all shapes and sizes. However, you may see some dogs with short tails, which have been surgically removed. This is called docking. It is done when the puppy is very young. The argument in favor of docking is that long tails left on working dogs are often injured when the animal is working. Today, though, docking is mostly done for fashion reasons.

Carried upright

Curled

Set high

Set low

Long, flowing

EARS

Dogs' distinctive ears can help you to identify them. However, in some countries the natural shape of the ear is altered by removing part of it so that the remaining part sticks up. This operation is called cropping. In some countries it is illegal.

Erect

Semi-erect

Pendent (hanging)

9

PEDIGREE

If a dog has ancestors of the same breed, which have been recorded for at least three generations, it is classed as a pedigree dog. Pedigree dogs have been bred for centuries, especially in the Far East and Middle East. Today, they are bred all over the world.

Pedigree registration is controlled by organizations such as kennel clubs. Pedigree breeders usually register puppies soon after they are born. If you buy a pedigree puppy, make sure that you are given its pedigree history, written on an official certificate, when you take it home.

Family tree of a pedigree Dalmatian

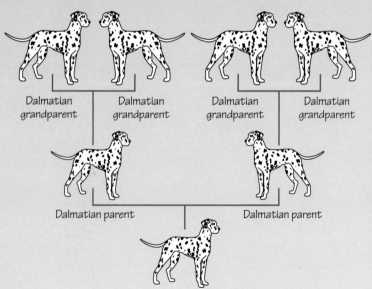

Dalmatian grandparent

Dalmatian grandparent

Dalmatian grandparent

Dalmatian grandparent

Dalmatian parent

Dalmatian parent

This dog can produce pedigree Dalmatians

CROSSBRED DOGS

If a dog's parents are of different breeds then it is called a crossbred dog. For example, if the father is a Golden Retriever and the mother is a German Shepherd, the dog is a Golden Retriever-German Shepherd cross.

Family tree of a cross-bred dog

Golden Retriever   German Shepherd

Cross-bred dog

MONGREL DOGS

A mongrel is a dog of mixed breed whose parents are either not known, or are themselves crossbred or mongrel.

Family tree of a mongrel

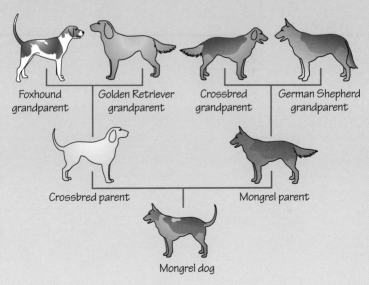

Foxhound grandparent   Golden Retriever grandparent   Crossbred grandparent   German Shepherd grandparent

Crossbred parent   Mongrel parent

Mongrel dog

TYPES OF DOG

GUARD DOGS
These dogs were originally bred to guard people and property. Some of them were used for hunting, too. They come from many parts of the world.

Boxer

HERDING DOGS
These dogs were bred to herd other animals – usually sheep or cattle. They were also used as guard dogs. Many are still used for herding in their places of origin.

Border Collie

GUN DOGS
Gun dogs were bred to help hunters. Some are used to find and chase out animals for hunters to shoot. Others are taught to fetch shot animals, usually birds.

Cocker Spaniel

HEELING DOGS
These little dogs were bred to drive cattle. If the cattle stop, the dogs nip their heels, then back off before the animal can kick. This is how they get their name.

Pembroke Corgi

RUNNING DOGS

Running dogs were bred to chase game. Different types have been bred all over the world, but they all share certain traits: they all have long legs, they are lightly built and they can run very fast.

Whippet

HAULING DOGS

These dogs were specially bred to pull sleds over snow and ice in the Arctic. Many are now popular pets. Some are still used to pull sleds for sport and fun.

Alaskan Malamute

SCENT HUNTERS

These dogs have a good sense of smell, which they use to hunt prey. In their home countries they are popular for hunting.

Wire-haired Dachshund

COMPANION DOGS

Dogs of this type were originally bred for a variety of uses. Their small size and friendliness made them popular as pets.

Pekingese

HUNTING TERRIERS

Hunting terriers were bred to chase animals such as foxes, badgers and rats.

Dandie Dinmont Terrier

GUARD DOGS

➡ KEESHOND
From Netherlands. Originally
used to guard barges, so
also called Dutch Barge
Dog. Good companion.
Fox-like head, and
neck ruff. Long
coat. Gray, with
cream legs and
feet. 16-19 inches.

"Spectacle"
markings
around
eyes

Feathering
on thighs

⬅ SCHIPPERKE
From Belgium. Also
called Belgian Barge
Dog. Loyal. Short,
smooth coat, longer
on neck. Usually
black. 12-13 inches.

➡ BULLDOG
British breed. Brave
and determined. Once
used for bull baiting. Big
head for body. Friendly.
Good watchdog. Short
coat. Any color, except
black. 12-14 inches.

Legs
wide apart

➡ BOXER
German breed. Very strong and active. Good guard, but fine house pet, too. Short, smooth coat. Can be red, fawn or brindle, often with white markings. 21-24 inches.

In the US, Boxers have cropped ears.

Docked tail

Big square head with prominent stop

◀ BULLMASTIFF
British, bred from Bulldog and Mastiff. Lively, loyal and fearless. Short coat. Red, fawn or brindle. 24-27 inches.

➡ ROTTWEILER
German. Used by police and armed forces. Intelligent but strong willed. Short coat. Black and tan. 22-27 inches.

15

GUARD DOGS

➡ GREAT DANE
First used in Germany,
France and Denmark,
to hunt wild boar.
Large but friendly. Will
guard. Short, smooth
coat. Fawn, black,
blue, brindle, or
harlequin. 29-32 inches.

Drooping, pendent
ears are cropped
in North America

Tail
held
low

In the US,
Dobermanns
have cropped ears.

Docked tail

⬅ DOBERMANN
German. Brave and loyal.
Needs training. Short
coat. Black, brown
or blue with tan
markings. 26-27 inches.

Ideally, the spots
should not overlap

➡ DALMATIAN
Thought to be
from Dalmatia,
Croatia. Lively and
friendly. Needs lots of
exercise. Short, sleek coat.
White, with black or liver
spots. 22-24 inches.

➡ ANATOLIAN KARABASH

From Turkey, where it was first used to guard sheep. Good guard, but needs training. Short coat. Cream, fawn, brindle or black. 26-30 inches.

⬅ LEONBERGER

Rare German breed. Friendly house dog and brave guard. Long, soft coat. Golden to red. 27-31 inches.

➡ ESTRELA MOUNTAIN DOG

From Estrela mountains, Portugal. Rare. Strong, intelligent and active. Usually fawn, black mask. 25-28 inches.

GUARD DOGS

➡ **NEWFOUNDLAND**
From Newfoundland, Canada. Good swimmer. Very strong, but gentle and friendly. Long coat. Black or bronze. 26-28 inches.

Pendent ears

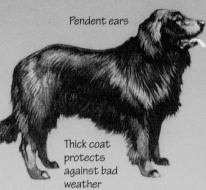

Thick coat protects against bad weather

Large head with square muzzle

⬅ **ST. BERNARD**
Bred by St. Bernard Hospice, Switzerland, to rescue travelers lost in snow. Heavy, strong but gentle. Rough or smooth coat. Usually red and white. 26-28 inches.

➡ **BERNESE MOUNTAIN DOG**
From Switzerland. Was used to pull carts. Easy to train. Long, soft coat. Black, brown or tan markings, white chest. 24-26 inches.

➡ GIANT SCHNAUZER

From Bavaria, Germany, where it was used to herd cattle. Energetic. Good guard dog, but needs training. Wiry coat. Black or salt and pepper. 28 inches.

Beard and whiskers

Docked tail

In the US, Standard Schnauzers have cropped ears.

Beard and whiskers

⬅ STANDARD SCHNAUZER

From Bavaria, Germany. Once used to kill rats and other pests. Lively, alert watch dog. Needs training. Wiry coat. Black or salt and pepper. 18-20 inches.

This dog's ears have been cropped

Beard and whiskers

Docked tail

➡ MINIATURE SCHNAUZER

From Bavaria, Germany. Loyal, active and alert. Rough, hard coat. Black or salt and pepper. 12-18 inches.

GUN DOGS

**➡ WELSH SPRINGER
SPANIEL**
Originally from Wales.
Smaller than English
Springer. Used for fetching
shot birds from water.
Lively, energetic pet.
Straight, thick, silky coat.
Red and white. 18-19 inches.

Docked
tail

**⬅ ENGLISH SPRINGER
SPANIEL**
Old spaniel breed. Finds,
drives out and retrieves
game. Active. Needs
regular exercise. Usually
liver and white, or black
and white. 20 inches.

Top-knot of
curly hair

Short,
smooth
tail tip

**➡ IRISH WATER
SPANIEL**
Old breed. Good at
retrieving game from
water. Playful and
active. Stiff, short curly
coat. Dark liver color.
20-23 inches.

➡ COCKER SPANIEL

British. Very popular show dog and pet. Intelligent, but needs lots of exercise. Medium to long coat. Many colors, such as black, red, liver or golden. 15-20 inches.

Long, drooping, pendent ears

Stop

Long, drooping, pendent ears

⬅ AMERICAN COCKER SPANIEL

Smaller than English Cocker. Lively. Coat feathered on body and legs. Thick coat needs regular grooming. Buff, black, or mixed colors. 14-16 inches.

Long, drooping, pendent ears

➡ FIELD SPANIEL

British. Friendly. Shorter legs, longer body than other Spaniels. Medium length coat. Most often black, red, liver or roan. 18 inches.

GUN DOGS

➡ SUSSEX SPANIEL

From England. Rare.
Active, friendly and
very easy to train.
Heavy body, with
short legs. Always
liver, with gold tips.
15-16 inches.

Docked tail

Docked
tail

Long,
heavy body

⬅ CLUMBER SPANIEL

From Clumber Park,
England. Strong and
friendly. Heavy, with
short legs. Close, silky
coat. White with lemon
markings. 19-20 inches.

Short legs

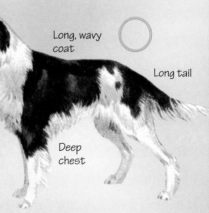

Long, wavy
coat

Long tail

➡ SMALL MÜNSTERLANDER

From Westphalia,
Germany. Used for
finding and retrieving
game. Friendly. White
and brown, with roan
marks. 19-22 inches.

Deep
chest

➡ CHESAPEAKE BAY RETRIEVER

Originally from East coast of USA. Intelligent, but strong willed and needs training. Dark brown to faded tan. 21-26 inches.

Short, slightly wavy coat

⬅ LABRADOR RETRIEVER

From Newfoundland, Canada, and named after Labrador, a region there. Popular gun dog, guide dog, police dog and pet. Black, chocolate or golden. 22-23 inches.

Short, thick coat

➡ CURLY-COATED RETRIEVER

British working dog. Strong gun dog. Can retrieve from water. Active, intelligent. Black or liver color. 25-27 inches.

Tightly curled coat

GUN DOGS

➡ FLAT-COATED RETRIEVER
British. Good retrieving dog. Strong and intelligent. Playful pet. Black or liver color. 20-24 inches.

Flat, springy coat

Feathering on tail and thighs

Feathering on front legs

Flat or wavy coat with feathering

⬅ GOLDEN RETRIEVER
Popular British breed. Works well. Good house dog, but needs lots of exercise. Any shade of cream or gold. 20-24 inches.

Docked tail

➡ WEIMARANER
From Weimar, Germany. Friendly, alert and active. Smooth coat. Silvery mouse-gray color. 22-25 inches.

Very short, fine coat

➤ ENGLISH SETTER

Old British breed. Good family pet. Black and white, lemon and white, liver and white, or tricolor. 24-27 inches.

Stop

Feathering on legs and tail

Long, silky, slightly wavy coat

◄ GORDON SETTER

Originally from Scotland. Heavy breed. Loyal, but tricky to train. Long, soft and glossy coat. Shiny black with tan markings. 26 inches.

Stop

➤ IRISH SETTER

From Ireland. Works well when trained. Very lively. Long neck and head. Long, silky coat. Always chestnut. 24 inches.

Deep chest

25

GUN DOGS

➡ VIZSLA
From Hungary. Finds and retrieves shot game birds. Gentle and affectionate, though very active. Short coat. Sandy yellow. 23-26 inches.

Long, drooping, pendent ears

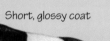
Short, glossy coat

⬅ POINTER
Originally from Spain. Points at game bird with nose, body and tail in straight line. Very active. Black, or another color with white. 24-27 inches.

Docked tail

➡ GERMAN SHORT-HAIRED POINTER
Finds and retrieves game. Friendly, but needs lots of exercise. Good guard. Liver, or liver and white spotted or flecked. 25-26 inches.

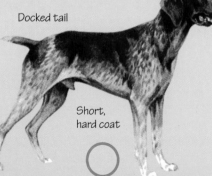
Short, hard coat

➡ DRENTSE PATRIJSHOND
From Netherlands. Good at
hunting partridge. Will
fetch game from water.
Thick, medium to long
coat. White, with
brown or orange.
22-25 inches.

Feathered
ears

Long,
feathered
tail

Fairly smooth coat

⬅ BRITTANY SPANIEL
Originally from Brittany,
France. Fast, intelligent.
Good pet. White, with
brown or orange.
18-20 inches.

Ears hang
flat

**➡ LARGE
MÜNSTERLANDER**
From Germany. Good
gun dog and pest
catcher. Active.
Needs training.
White with black
patches.
23-25 inches.

Long,
slightly
wavy coat

27

HERDING DOGS

➡ MAREMMA
From Central Italy.
Good herder and
guard. Intelligent,
though independent.
Black nose. Usually
white, can have lemon
or fawn markings.
24-30 inches.

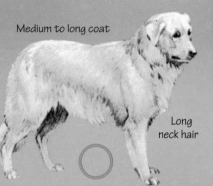

Medium to long coat

Long
neck hair

Long
neck
hair

Short, wavy
body hair

⬅ KUVASZ
From Hungary. Used
for guarding sheep
and cattle. Loyal and
protective. Always
white. 27-30 inches.

Thick coat

**⬅ GREAT
PYRENEES**
From Pyrenees
mountains on the
French-Spanish border.
Guards sheep. Large
and strong, though
gentle. All white, or
white with markings.
26-32 inches.

➡ BELGIAN SHEEP DOG

Sheepdog from Belgium.
Intelligent and obedient.
Very good watch dog.
Fairly long coat. Black.
23-25 inches.

Triangular, erect ears

Long neck hair

Triangular, erect ears

⬅ MALINOIS

Belgian Shepherd Dog.
Smooth coat, similar to
German Shepherd Dog.
Fawn or red coloring,
with black hair tips.
23-25 inches.

➡ TERVUEREN

From Belgium. Looks like
Belgian Sheep Dog, but is
reddish-fawn with black
hair tips and tail tip.
23-25 inches.

29

HERDING DOGS

➡ GERMAN SHEPHERD DOG
Used by police, armed
forces and as guide dog
for blind. Intelligent,
loyal and easy to
train. Any color.
22-26 inches.

Triangular,
erect ears

Tail hangs in
slight curve

Smooth
coat

Long outer
coat

Full neck
ruff

Semi-erect
ears

⬅ ROUGH COLLIE
Originally from Scotland,
where it was used to herd
sheep. Friendly and active.
Needs regular grooming.
Colors are sable and white, blue
merle, tricolor, white (with
colored head or body parts)
24-27 inches.

Semi-erect
ears

➡ SMOOTH COLLIE
British. Less common
than Rough Collie.
Has a short, smooth,
hard coat.
20-24 inches.

➡ OLD ENGLISH SHEEPDOG

Often called "bobtail." Good guard dog. Strong and active. Needs daily grooming. Gray, blue or grizzle, with or without white. Over 22 inches.

Ears lie flat on head

No tail

Beard on both sides of muzzle

⬅ BEARDED COLLIE

Originally from Scotland. Mainly used as sheepdog. Loyal, loving pet. Long coat. Can be blue, gray-black, red and white. 20-22 inches.

➡ SHETLAND SHEEPDOG

Originally from Shetland Islands, Scotland. Looks like small Rough Collie. Ideal family pet. Colors include black, blue, merle and sable. 14-15 inches.

Semi-erect ears

Full neck ruff

HERDING DOGS

➡ TIBETAN TERRIER
From mountains of Tibet. Once used to herd sheep, goats and cattle. Lively, active and intelligent. Long, fine double coat. White, cream, gray, golden and black. 14-16 inches.

Tail curled over back

Large, round feet

Tail curled over back

Corded coat

⬅ PULI
From Hungary. Wooly undercoat. Long outer coat hangs in cords and needs regular attention. Can work in cold conditions. White, gray or black. 15-18 inches.

➡ KOMONDOR
From Hungary. Thick coat hangs in long cords. Bold, hard worker. Loyal, protective companion. Always white. 22-33 inches.

Corded coat

Hair falls over eyes

Curved tail

➡ BORDER COLLIE
Good working sheepdog, from northern England. Very intelligent and energetic. Needs regular, hard exercise. Medium to long, smooth or slightly wavy coat. Usually black and white. 20-21 inches.

Eyebrows hang over eyes

⬇ BRIARD
French breed. Intelligent and active. Square look to body. Can be any color apart from white. 22-23 inches.

Feathered, curved tail

Docked tail

➡ BOUVIER DES FLANDRES
Bred in Flanders, Belgium, to herd cattle. Active. Rough, wiry coat. Has eyebrows, beard and moustache. Drab yellow, gray or black. 24-27 inches.

HEELING DOGS

➡ KELPIE
Australian. Bred from
sheepdogs. Hard working.
Tough and active. Short
coat. Black, red
or chocolate.
17-20 inches.

Erect
ears

Tail curled
over back and
to one side

⬅ NORWEGIAN BUHUND
Farm dog. Brave and
intelligent. Long, thick coat,
which is longest on body
and neck. Fawn, red
or yellowish. 18 inches.

Speckled
coat

**➡ AUSTRALIAN
CATTLE DOG**
Bred from Smooth Collie,
dingo (wild dog) and
Dalmatian. Tough. Used for
driving cattle. Short coat.
Red or blue speckled.
18-20 inches.

➡ VALLHUND

From Sweden.
Also called
"Västgötaspets."
Almost died out in
1940s. Has short coat.
Can be gray, brownish
or red. 15-20 inches.

Very short
tail

Erect ears

Short
coat

⬅ PEMBROKE CORGI

Originally used to drive
cattle and ponies in
South Wales. Now a
popular pet. Will nip.
Can be red, black,
fawn, black or tan.
Can have white
markings. 10-12 inches.

Large, erect
ears point out

➡ CARDIGAN CORGI

Another driving dog
from South Wales.
Longer body and
larger ears than
Pembroke. Short
coat. Will nip. Any
color except
all-white. 12 inches.

Tail looks like
fox's brush

RUNNING DOGS

➡ SALUKI
Bred in Middle East to hunt deer
and antelope. Loyal and active.
Long ears. White, golden, black
and tan. 23-28 inches.

Smooth coat

Feathered,
curved tail

Feathered
legs

⬅ SLOUGHI
Bred in North Africa to hunt small
game. Rare. Looks like smooth
Saluki. Active. Usually sandy, can
be brindle. 22-30 inches.

Feathered
tail

➡ BORZOI
Bred in Russia to hunt
game and wolves.
Active and friendly.
Various colors.
28-32 inches.

Long, silky
coat

Long tail,
curved
at tip

⬅ AFGHAN HOUND
Bred in Afghanistan to
hunt deer. Long, silky
coat, feathered ears.
All colors. 26-30 inches.

➡ IRISH WOLFHOUND

Irish breed. One of largest
breeds. Good natured.
Rough, hard coat. Gray,
brindle, red, fawn, black
or pure white. Over 28 inches.

⬅ DEERHOUND

Scottish breed. Smaller and
lighter than Irish Wolfhound.
Once used to hunt deer. Thick,
rough coat. Gray, yellowish
or brindle. 28-30 inches.

➡ PHARAOH HOUND

Ancient breed. Probably
North African. Smooth
coat. Often rich red, with
white on chest. 21-25 inches.

Large,
erect ears

⬅ IBIZAN HOUND

From island of Ibiza, Spain. Used
as hunter and watch dog. Rough
or smooth coat. 24-26 inches.

RUNNING DOGS

➡ GREYHOUND
Ancient breed, used for
hunting hares and rabbits.
Very fast. Will chase small
animals. Now used for
track racing. Smooth
coat. Most colors.
28-30 inches.

Long, low-
set tail

Deep
chest

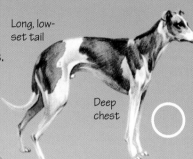

⬅ LURCHER
Gypsies' traditional hunting
dog. Usually greyhound-collie
cross. Rough coated. Fawn,
gray or black. 28-30 inches.

➡ WHIPPET
Originally from northern
England. Bred for racing.
Looks like miniature greyhound.
Friendly. Smooth coat. Any
color or color mix. 18-20 inches.

Semi-erect ears
fold back

Curved back

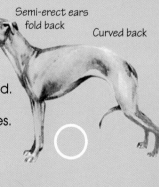

Semi-erect ears
folded back

Arched
back

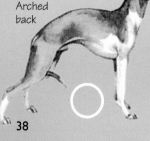

⬅ ITALIAN GREYHOUND
Originally from Italy. Smallest
running dog. Quiet and friendly.
Smooth coat. Fawn, black,
cream, white, pied. 13-14 inches.

HAULING DOGS

➡ ALASKAN MALAMUTE
From northern Canada. Large, strong dog. Loves people, but can be aggressive to other dogs. Gray to black, white under body. 23-28 inches.

Mask-like markings on head

Thick coat

Tail curves over back

⬅ SIBERIAN HUSKY
From Siberia, northern Russia. Used for herding, sled pulling. Good worker. Friendly pet. Long, thick, soft coat. All colors, with white markings. 20-24 inches.

Small, erect ears

Tail curves over back

➡ SAMOYED
Russian breed. Still used in sled races. Can round up reindeer. Good pet. Silver-white. May have cream marks. 18-21 inches.

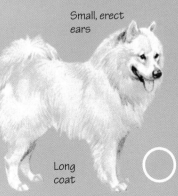

Long coat

39

SCENT HUNTERS

➤ FINNISH SPITZ
Originally from Finland, where it was used for hunting. Good guard. Noisy. Medium to long coat. Red-gold to red-brown. 16-18 inches.

Erect, pointed ears

Tightly-curled tail

◀ ELKHOUND
Originally from Norway, where it was used to hunt elk. Can stand cold weather. Independent, energetic. Thick, hard coat. Gray. 19-21 inches.

Ridge of hairs on back

➤ RHODESIAN RIDGEBACK
From Rhodesia (now Zimbabwe), Africa. Used for guarding and hunting. Strong fighter. Short, glossy coat. Yellowish to reddish. 24-27 inches.

40

➤ BASSET GRIFFON VENDÉEN

From southwestern France, where it was used for hunting hares. Active. Mostly white, with markings. 14-17 inches.

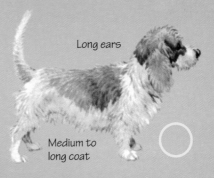

Long ears

Medium to long coat

Tail carried high

← BEAGLE

English breed. Originally used for hunting. Active. Very friendly pet. Short, hard coat. Various colors. 14-16 inches.

➤ BASSET HOUND

French breed. Good natured. Lively. Smooth, short coat. Various colors. 13-15 inches.

Very long, pendent ears

➤ BASENJI

From central Africa. Originally used to hunt antelope. Very friendly. Black, red, chestnut and white, or black and tan with white. 16-17 inches.

Tail tightly curled

SCENT HUNTERS

➡ BLOODHOUND
Ancient breed, from
Normandy, northern
France. Great sense
of smell. Used to hunt
deer and track scent
of escaped prisoners.
Short, glossy coat.
Black or liver and
tan, sometimes red.
24-26 inches.

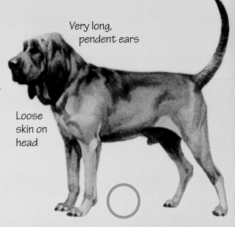

Very long, pendent ears

Loose skin on head

Long tail

⬅ FOXHOUND
Used in packs for hunting,
especially in Britain. Friendly.
Short, smooth coat. Usually
tan, with black and white
markings, or white with black,
tan or lemon marks. 21-25
inches.

➡ OTTERHOUND
British breed, originally
to hunt otters. Swims
well. Medium to long,
hard coat. Usually fawn or
gray with black and tan
markings. 24-26 inches.

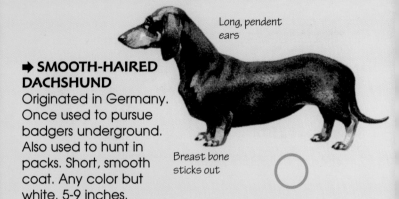

Long, pendent ears

Breast bone sticks out

➡ SMOOTH-HAIRED DACHSHUND

Originated in Germany. Once used to pursue badgers underground. Also used to hunt in packs. Short, smooth coat. Any color but white. 5-9 inches.

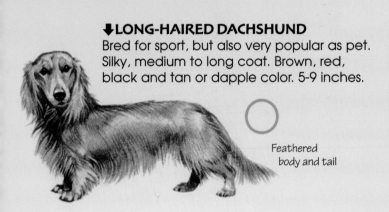

⬇LONG-HAIRED DACHSHUND

Bred for sport, but also very popular as pet. Silky, medium to long coat. Brown, red, black and tan or dapple color. 5-9 inches.

Feathered body and tail

⬇ WIRE-HAIRED DACHSHUND

Has been used to hunt wild boar and follow other game underground. Short coat. All colors. 5-9 inches.

Eyebrows

Feathered body and tail

Beard

43

COMPANION DOGS

➡ CHOW CHOW
Originally bred in China. Popular pet. Looks a little like a lion. Alert and independent. Black, red, blue, fawn or cream in color. 18-22 inches.

Tail curls over hip

⬅ PUG
From China. Was popular with English royal family in 1800s. Very loving pet. Short, glossy coat. Fawn or black. 13 inches.

➡ LÖWCHEN
Probably comes from the Mediterranean. Also called "Little Lion Dog." Ancient, rare breed. Long coat. Friendly. Usually black, white, gray or cream. 10 inches.

Tufted tail

Clipped coat

Crest of hair

⬅ CHINESE CRESTED DOG
Despite its name, probably from Mexico or Africa, not China. Almost hairless. Patches of pink, blue, mauve or white. 13 inches.

➡ KING CHARLES SPANIEL
Favorite at court of King
Charles II of England. Gentle
and loving. Long, silky coat.
Black and tan, rich
red or tricolor. 10-11 inches.

Short
muzzle

Long,
feathered
ears

⬅ CAVALIER KING CHARLES SPANIEL
Long, silky coat. Larger
than King Charles Spaniel.
Friendly. Black and tan, red
and white, red or tricolor.
12-13 inches.

➡ TIBETAN SPANIEL
First bred by monks
of Tibet. Looks like
a Pekingese. Long,
smooth coat. Golden,
cream, white, black,
or tricolor. 10-11 inches.

Curled tail

⬅ BICHON FRISE
Probably from Spain.
Friendly. Silky white coat,
often with gray patches
on skin. 8-12 inches.

COMPANION DOGS

➡ JAPANESE CHIN
Probably originated in China, but became the pet of many Japanese emperors. Long coat. White with red or black patches. 12 inches.

Rounded skull

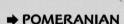

⬅ PAPILLON
First bred in France. Called "Butterfly Dog" because of shape of its head and ears. Long coat. White with all colors except liver. 11 inches.

Tail lies flat over back

➡ POMERANIAN
From Pomerania, Germany/Poland. Small version of Finnish Spitz. Red, blue, orange, white, black or brown. 11 inches.

⬅ AFFENPINSCHER
Tiny dog, from Germany. Often shown in old Dutch paintings. Looks a little like a monkey. Wiry coat, usually black. Up to 11 inches.

➡ SHIH TZU
Originally from China. Tiny but brave. Rounded skull, square muzzle. Playful. Long straight coat. All colors. Up to 11 inches.

Beard and whiskers

Tail curls over back

⬅ MALTESE
Very old breed, from Malta. Often painted in pictures as lap dog. Loyal. Short body and legs. Long, pure white coat. 8-10 inches.

➡ PEKINGESE
Originally from China, where it was once a court pet. Long coat. Stubborn. All colors except liver. 6-10 inches.

Tail curled over back

⬅ LHASA APSO
Originally from Tibet. Lively and assertive. Long, hard coat. Usually golden, sandy or gray. 10-11 inches.

COMPANION DOGS

➡ AUSTRALIAN SILKY TERRIER
Bred in Australia from Yorkshire and Australian Terriers. Long, silky coat. Silver, or blue with tan marks. 9 inches.

Small, erect ears

Very long coat with parting in middle

⬅ YORKSHIRE TERRIER
Tiny English Terrier. Very popular pet. Good rat and mouse catcher. Long, straight, silky coat. Should be dark blue and tan colored. 7-8 inches.

➡ GRIFFON BRUXELLOIS
Originally from Belgium. Lively little dog. Rough, wiry, short coat. Red, black or black and tan. 7-8 inches.

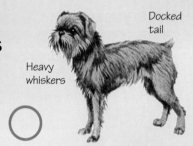

Docked tail

Heavy whiskers

➡ GRIFFON BRABANÇON
From Belgium. Similar to Griffon Bruxellois, but smooth-coated. Also called "Smooth Griffon." 7-8 inches.

Docked tail

➡ CHIHUAHUA, SMOOTH-COAT

Mexican. Smallest breed. Also called "Ornament Dog" or "Pillow Dog." Bold. Can be aggressive. Fine coat. 6-9 inches.

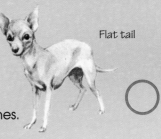

Flat tail

⬅ CHIHUAHUA, LONG-COAT

Silky coat with feathering. Same stature and character as smooth-coated version. Can be any color. 6-9 inches.

➡ POODLES

Probably originated in Germany. Easy to train. Coat curly, hard and thick. Any color. Split into categories: "Toy," "Miniature" and "Standard." Category sizes vary according to different rules of various kennel clubs around the world.

Standard

Coats have been trimmed into "lion cut"

Toy

Miniature

COMPANION DOGS

➤ FRENCH BULLDOG
Has large ears, which look like a bat's. Very friendly little dog. Short coat. Brindle, fawn or pied. 10-14 inches.

Docked tail | White collar

◀ BOSTON TERRIER
Originally from the USA. Lively and clever. Short, glossy coat. Broad, round head. Brindle and white, or black and white. 16 inches.

➤ TOY MANCHESTER TERRIER
Also called "Black and Tan." Miniature version of Manchester Terrier. Brave and alert. Good rat hunter. Smooth, short coat. Black and tan. 10-12 inches.

Docked tail

◀ MINIATURE PINSCHER
German breed. Lively and spirited, but easily trained. Short, smooth coat. Red, black, blue or chocolate with tan markings. 10-12 inches.

50

HUNTING TERRIERS

➡ MANCHESTER TERRIER
Originally from Manchester,
northern England, where
it was used to catch rats.
Intelligent and lively. Short,
glossy coat. Black and tan.
15-16 inches.

Short, glossy coat

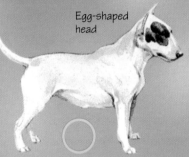

Egg-shaped
head

⬅ BULL TERRIER
English breed. Friendly
to people, but fights dogs.
Short, smooth coat. White,
sometimes with markings,
or colored. 14-16 inches.

**➡ STAFFORDSHIRE
BULL TERRIER**
From Staffordshire, England.
Short, glossy coat. Very friendly
with people, but loves to fight
other dogs. Red, fawn, blue
or black. 14-16 inches.

Semi-erect
ears

Short
legs

**⬅ PARSON'S RUSSELL
TERRIER**
British. Bred from several
different types of terriers.
Excellent pest catcher. Short
or rough-coated. White with
colored patches. 9-15 inches.

TERRIERS

➡ WEST HIGHLAND TERRIER
Originally from Scotland. Popular house pet. Good guard. Long, coarse coat, soft undercoat. Always white. Up to 11 inches.

Small, upright tail

⬅ SCOTTISH TERRIER
Once called "Aberdeen Terrier." Show dog and pet. Intelligent. Wiry, medium to long coat. Black, flecked gray or brown. 10-11 inches.

➡ SEALYHAM TERRIER
Originally from Wales, where it was used for hunting in packs. Long, wiry coat. White, sometimes with yellow markings on head and ears. 12 inches.

Slightly curved head

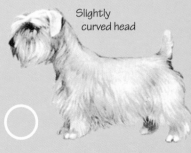

➡ CAIRN TERRIER
Originally from Scotland. Similar to West Highland. Medium to long, hard coat. Red, sandy, gray, mottled brown or off-black. 10-11 inches.

Small, pointed, erect ears

➡ NORWICH TERRIER AND NORFOLK TERRIER

British breeds, very similar to one another. Norwich has erect ears, Norfolk has semi-erect ears. Wiry coat. Red, black and tan, sandy or grayish color. 10 inches.

Docked tail

Erect ears

⬅ BORDER TERRIER

Very active breed. Rough, weatherproof coat. Red, wheaten, gray and tan or blue and tan color. 10-12 inches.

➡ DANDIE DINMONT TERRIER

Named after character in a book by Sir Walter Scott. Coat of mixed soft and hard hairs. Pepper or mustard color. 8-11 inches.

Large, wide head

⬅ AUSTRALIAN TERRIER

Popular in Australia and New Zealand. Strong and friendly. Hard, straight coat. Red, or blue and tan in color. 10 inches.

Docked tail

53

TERRIERS

➡ AIREDALE TERRIER
Named after Aire Valley,
Yorkshire, England. Largest
terrier. Bred to hunt pests.
Srong but easy to train.
Rough, wiry coat. Black
or gray and tan.
22-24inches.

⬅ LAKELAND TERRIER
From northern England.
Used for hunting. Friendly.
Rough, thick coat. Various
colors. 15 inches.

➡ WELSH TERRIER
Used in Wales to hunt. Strong.
Good guard dog and house
dog. Hard, wiry coat. Black
and tan. 16 inches.

Semi-erect
ears carried
forward

Beard and
whiskers

Beard
and
whiskers

⬅ KERRY BLUE TERRIER
Irish. Bred to hunt foxes,
badgers and otters. Popular
show dog. Soft wavy coat.
Any blue shade. 18-19 inches.

➡ IRISH TERRIER

From Ireland. Likes to fight, but friendly to people. Fairly short coat. Any shade of red. 18 inches.

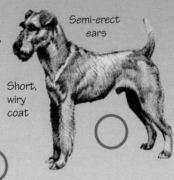

Semi-erect ears

Short, wiry coat

Top knot

Arched back

⬅ BEDLINGTON TERRIER

From northern England. Looks a little like a lamb. Brave and friendly. Good pet. Thick, wavy coat. Blue, liver, sandy or mixed colors. 16 inches.

➡ FOX TERRIER, SMOOTH-COAT

From England. Lively and intelligent. Short, hard, smooth coat. Mainly white. 15-16 inches.

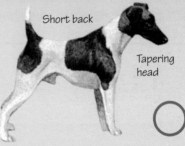

Short back

Tapering head

Short back

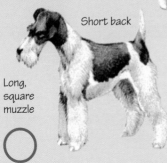

Long, square muzzle

⬅ FOX TERRIER, WIRE-COAT

Similar to Smooth-coat, but with longer, wiry hair. White, some black or tan markings. 15-16 inches.

CHOOSING A DOG

Dogs can be fantastic companions, and great fun. However, they need a lot of looking after. Make sure that you will be able to commit lots of time and energy to taking care of your dog.

Find out as much as you can about the different breeds. Choose a dog that is the right size and temperament to suit your lifestyle.

PUPPIES

Choose a puppy that is friendly to you. However, beware of any that are too bold, they may be hard to train. Similarly, watch out for very shy ones, they may stay nervous all their lives.

If you want to buy a puppy, look for signs that it is healthy. The picture below shows some of the things to look for.

Check that the coat is healthy. A poor coat can be a sign of hard-to-treat skin problems.

Inspect the ears. Dirty ears are a clue that the pup may be ill.

Bright eyes are a sign of good general health.

Look for a full set of teeth. Bad teeth may signal illness.